Men-at-Arms • 562

Partisan Warfare in Greece 1941–44

Phoebus Athanassiou • Illustrated by Adam Hook

Series editors Martin Windrow & Nick Reynolds

OSPREY PUBLISHING
Bloomsbury Publishing Plc
Kemp House, Chawley Park, Cumnor Hill, Oxford OX2 9PH, UK
Bloomsbury Publishing Ireland Limited,
29 Earlsfort Terrace, Dublin 2, D02 AY28, Ireland
1385 Broadway, 5th Floor, New York, NY 10018, USA
E-mail: info@ospreypublishing.com
www.ospreypublishing.com

OSPREY is a trademark of Osprey Publishing Ltd

First published in Great Britain in 2025

A catalogue record for this book is available from the British Library.

ISBN: PB 9781472867520; eBook 9781472867537;
ePDF 9781472867506; XML 9781472867513

25 26 27 28 29   10 9 8 7 6 5 4 3 2 1

Index by Rob Munro
Typeset by PDQ Digital Media Solutions, Bungay, UK
Printed by Repro India Ltd.

MIX
Paper
FSC   FSC® C047271

Osprey Publishing supports the Woodland Trust, the UK's leading woodland
conservation charity.

To find out more about our authors and books visit **www.ospreypublishing.com**.
Here you will find extracts, author interviews, details of forthcoming events and
the option to sign up for our newsletter.

For product safety related questions contact productsafety@bloomsbury.com

Dedication

This book is dedicated to my maternal grandparents, Eleni and Efstathios, who
survived Greece's triple occupation, and to all those who did not.

Acknowledgements

For their support and help in the preparation of this book, the author is grateful
to Ms Elena Antonakaki, of the Photographic Archives of the Athens War
Museum; Ms Zanet Battinou and Ms Anastasia Loudarou, of the Jewish
Museum of Greece; Mr Pericles Kapetanopoulos, Director of the Helioupolis
National Resistance Museum; Mr Athanassios Koskinas, of the EAM National
Resistance Museum of Kessariani; Dr Iason Chandrinos, of the University of
Regensburg; and, finally, to Ms Andra Florian.

Author's note

In the absence of any commonly accepted and widely used transliteration rules
for the rendition of Greek characters and diphthongs into Latin script, the
transliteration approach opted for in the text is the one corresponding best to
the phonetics of the relevant Greek characters and diphthongs.

Artist's note

Readers may care to note that the original paintings from which the colour
plates in this book were prepared are available for private sale. All reproduction
copyright whatsoever is retained by the publishers. All enquiries should be
addressed to:

scorpiopaintings@btinternet.com

The publishers regret that they can enter into no correspondence upon
this matter.

Title-page photograph: A group of ELAS guerrillas pose for the camera in
Livadeia with an assortment of semi-automatic weapons, including two British
Sten Mk II (first and third from the left), a German MP 35/I (second from the left)
and a Soviet PPSh-41 (first from the right). (Iason Chandrinos Collection)

Abbreviations used in the text

AAA: Agon-Anorthosis-Apeleftherosis (Rebirth and Liberation Struggle)
EAM: Ethniko Apeleftherotiko Metopo (National Liberation Front)
EAO: Ethnikes Antartikes Omades (National Guerrilla Bands)
EDES: Ethnikos Dimokratikos Ellinikos Syndesmos (National Republican
Greek League)
EES: Ethnikos Ellinikos Stratos (National Greek Army)
EKKA: Ethniki kai Koinoniki Apeleftherosis (National and Social Liberation)
ELAN: Elliniko Laiko Apeleftherotiko Naftiko (Hellenic Popular Liberation Navy)
ELAS: Ethnikos Laikos Apeleftherotikos Stratos (National Popular Liberation Army)
EOEA: Ethnikes Omades Ellinon Antarton (National Bands of Greek Guerrillas)
EPON: Eniaia Panelladiki Organosi Neon (United Panhellenic Youth Organization)
KKE: Kommounistiko Komma Ellados (Communist Party of Greece)
PAO: Panellinios Apeleftherotiki Organosis (Panhellenic Liberation Organization)
PEEA: Politiki Epitropi Ethnikis Apeleftherosis (Political Committee for
National Liberation)
YBE: Yperaspistes Boreiou Ellados (Defenders of Northern Greece)

PARTISAN WARFARE IN GREECE 1941–44

INTRODUCTION

On 6 April 1941, troops assigned to Germany's 12. Armee (Generalfeldmarschall Wilhelm von List) crossed the Greco-Bulgarian border, invading Greece. The German intervention served a triple objective: to break the bloody stalemate into which the Greek Army (Ellinikós Stratós) had fought Italy's Royal Army (*Regio Esercito*) following Mussolini's ill-fated invasion of Greece (28 October 1940); to secure Germany's south-eastern flank in anticipation of the planned invasion of the Soviet Union; and to secure bases for the Luftwaffe to strike against British forces along the Eastern Mediterranean and in North Africa. Faced with a two-front war, in an area extending from the Adriatic Sea to the Greco-Bulgarian border, the Greek Army and the Allied Expeditionary Corps – mostly consisting of Australian and New Zealand troops hurriedly sent to Greece from the North African front – staged a fighting retreat south before succumbing to the Wehrmacht's inexorable superiority. The Germans had reached Athens by 27 April and the southernmost shores of mainland Greece by 30 April. By the end of May they had also captured Crete, following an intense, 13-day-long struggle involving the large-scale deployment of airborne troops. The fall of Crete signalled the end of Greece's sovereignty and the start of the country's *Katochì* (occupation), a dark period that was to last three long years.

German Flak troops (including a Luftwaffe NCO, scanning the sky with his binoculars) man a 3.7cm anti-aircraft gun in the centre of Athens, against the backdrop of Mount Lycabettus. This photograph was taken in late May 1941, when the Axis forces were still in the process of consolidating their grip on Greece, and when the threat of British air raids was still perceived as real. Owing to the early-morning heat, some of the gun crew have stripped down to the bare essentials. (Author's Collection)

A column of Bulgarian troops crosses into Greece, in April or May 1941, following Germany's invasion and the collapse of the Greek defences. The troops visible here all wear the Bulgarian Army's *bustina*-type forage cap rather than steel helmets, suggesting that they do not expect to encounter resistance as they head south. (Author's Collection)

The Axis Powers divided Greece into three occupation zones. Germany controlled the most strategically important areas; Bulgaria occupied (and annexed) eastern Macedonia, western Thrace and the islands of Thassos and Samothraki; and Italy took over the remainder of the Greek mainland, eastern Crete (Lasithi prefecture), and the south Aegean Sea and Ionian Sea islands. Germany and Italy jointly occupied Athens and the port city of Piraeus. An Allied naval blockade of Greece and the requisition of foodstuffs by the occupation forces were to lead, already in the first winter of occupation, to the Great Famine, which ravaged Athens and other large urban centres. The combination of food shortages, rampant hyperinflation, and high-handedness on the part of the Axis occupiers led to growing public discontent and resentment, especially in the cities, where living conditions were harsher and repression more systematic. The scene was set for resistance. By October 1944, Greece's armed resistance movement had grown into one of the largest in occupied Europe, with well over 100,000 armed *andartes* (partisans), out of a total population of barely 7.5 million.

This book aims to provide as comprehensive an account of partisan warfare in Greece as space constraints will allow, with an emphasis on the forces involved in it, their organization and tactics.

A delegation of senior Wehrmacht officers on a visit to the Acropolis, have their picture taken before the Erechtheion, on 10 May 1941. The Wehrmacht entered Athens – previously declared an open city – on 27 April 1941, initiating a three year-long period of harsh occupation and resistance against the Axis forces. (Author's Collection)

GREECE'S TRADITIONS OF IRREGULAR WARFARE

Modern-day Greece gained its independence from the Ottoman Empire in 1829. From a tactical perspective, the Greek War of Independence (1821–29) bore many of the hallmarks of a guerrilla war, pitting lightly armed bands of locally recruited irregulars, often tied by links of blood and kinship to one another and to their chieftains, against a numerically stronger and conventionally organized regular military force. Exploiting the topography and their superior knowledge of the terrain, and deploying ruses, the insurgents harassed Ottoman troops, springing ambushes on them and staging small- and medium-scale actions with the objective of wearing down and, ultimately, defeating their more conventionally organized rivals.

Banditry remained endemic in the Greek countryside for the whole of the 19th century and into the 20th, keeping alive the flame of guerrilla warfare (piracy, its seaborne equivalent, had been extinguished soon after the creation of the Kingdom of Greece in 1832). Greece's human geography, with its large, poor and hardy rural population, was a further contributory factor to the endemic banditry phenomenon. Many were those who idealized brigands as bearers of a time-honoured tradition of martial individualism and romanticized resistance to oppression. Socio-economic and historical considerations aside, what contributed to the spread and perseverance of banditry across Greece was the country's difficult topography: its mountainous and rugged terrain, extensive woodlands and poor road network provided ample hiding spaces for outlaws, rendering their detection and neutralization a challenging task.

In 1941, the people of Greece were less indigent and backward in their *mores* than their forefathers, but they had at least three good reasons to be partial towards armed resistance. First, they had access to a repository of weapons and to a modest supply of ammunition that Greek soldiers had secreted following the collapse of their tenacious defence in the Pindus Mountains and along the Macedonian border (in recognition of their valour, the Germans had not interned Greek soldiers, nor had they disarmed their officers). Second, they were emboldened by the precedent of their near-defeat of Fascist Italy, free Europe's first noteworthy land warfare success against the Axis. Third, they could count on an organization with an unparalleled capital of experience in clandestine, conspiratorial activities: the KKE, the patron of EAM-ELAS, Greece's largest and most potent armed resistance movement.

Two unidentified *andartes* pose for the camera. Judging by the costume of the *andartis* on the left and, in particular, by his headdress and legwear, widely worn by the peasants on either side of Greece's northern border, this picture was most likely taken in western Macedonia or Thrace. The *andartis* on the right seems to be armed with the reliable 6.5mm Mannlicher-Schönauer M1903/14 rifle, the standard-issue infantry weapon of the former Royal Greek Army. (Athens War Museum)

RESISTANCE IN GREECE

The struggle between the two extremes of the national armed resistance movement was one of the defining features of partisan warfare in Greece. At one end stood ELAS, the military arm of EAM, a KKE-dominated loose coalition of pre-war left-wing political parties, all but uprooted in the run-up to the Greco-Italian War (1940–41) by the repressive regime of Ioannis Metaxas (August 1936–January 1941). At the opposite end stood EDES, the brainchild of a group of Athens-based Republican-minded political and military figures.

What ELAS and EDES had in common at the time of their formation was their anti-Monarchist agenda (at the start of the National Resistance, all major Greek political parties opposed monarchy, which they considered responsible for the pre-war Metaxas dictatorship). As the National Resistance dragged on, these two guerrilla bands became increasingly radicalized: EDES shed its Republican stance and turned pro-Monarchist, while ELAS became more unabashed about its fundamentally Communist orientation. In the case of EDES, the shift away from its more liberal origins was an act of political expediency, as its main lifeline, Britain, actively sponsored the unpopular King George II of the Hellenes (r. 1922–24; 1935–47) and his Cairo-based government-in-exile, vehemently opposing any attempt to abolish the monarchy. In the case of ELAS, its Communist epiphany was an expression of its true colours, as EAM, its patron, was controlled by the KKE, the only organized political force in the country with an ideological foundation strong enough, and a clandestine network effective enough, to mount a nationwide insurgency against the Axis. The radicalization of the two main agents of the Greek resistance movement laid the ground for an internecine showdown that was to prove every bit as dramatic as the fight against Axis occupation.

CHRONOLOGY

1941

6 April German forces invade Greece via Bulgaria (Operation *Marita*), occupying Athens on 27 April.

20 May–1 June German airborne troops capture Crete (Operation *Merkur*).

16 July KKE establishes EAM.

29 September In reprisals for the Drama uprising, Bulgarian troops execute all 485 male inhabitants of the town of Doxato.

15 October Establishment of EDES.

December Start of the 'Great Famine', costing an estimated 270,000 lives.

1942

April EAM establishes ELAS as its military arm.

23 July Colonel Napoleon Zervas takes to the mountains of north-western Greece (Epirus), in charge of the first nucleus of EDES guerrillas.

30 September Lieutenant-Colonel E.C.W. Myers leads a 12-strong British party into Greece, with orders to enlist the help of guerrilla groups and cut the north–south railway line.

24–25 November Destruction of the Gorgopotamos River railway bridge by 12 British operators and 150 ELAS and EDES *andartes* (Operation *Harling*).

1943

16 February Myers receives instructions to organize and equip the *andartes* throughout Greece, and to prepare sabotage plans (21 February).

23 February EPON, occupied Greece's largest youth resistance organization, is established.

1 March ELAS bands capture Colonel Stéfanos Saráfis and disperse his band; start of the mass deportation of the Jews of Thessaloniki to the Auschwitz death camp.

April–May Ioannis Rallis, the newly appointed head of the puppet government, establishes the first state-sponsored armed collaborationist troops; Colonel Dimitrios Psarros sets up EKKA around Mount Parnassus; Colonel Saráfis assumes the military command of ELAS.

2 May Establishment of the ELAS GHQ, signifying the transformation of ELAS from a rebel force into a regular army.

June Negotiation of the National Bands Agreement between ELAS and EDES; destruction of the Asopos River railway bridge by a six-strong British party (20–21 June).

September Armistice of Cassibile, leading to Italy's exit from World War II (3 September); German forces launch Operation *Achse*, to disarm the Italian armed forces in Greece (8 September); Italy's 24ª Divisione di fanteria 'Pinerolo' and the Reggimento 'Lancieri di Aosta' (6°) go over to ELAS (12 September); German forces disarm Italy's 33ª Divisione di fanteria 'Acqui', stationed on Cephalonia, executing some 5,000 of its personnel (22 September).

October German forces launch Operation *Panther* against guerrilla forces in the Metsovon Pass, Mount Olympos, Mount Parnassus, Ioannina and the Amfissa areas of Greece; German forces capture the island of Kos, taking 2,500 Italian and 600 British soldiers prisoner and executing 96 Italian officers (4 October); ELAS attacks rival bands in Epirus and Thessaly (9–31 October); battle of Vourgarelli (Tzoumerka Mountains) pits EDES forces against elements of the 1. Gebirgs-Division (30–31 October); EDES negotiates 'silent' ceasefire with the XXII. Gebirgskorps (end of October).

16 November The Italian garrison of Leros, and 3,200 British troops, surrender to German forces.

December EDES withdraws to a small area of Epirus, to re-group; the Kalavryta Massacre (13 December) conducted by men of the 117. Jäger-Division results in 693 civilian casualties, including women and children.

1944

February ELAS and EDES agree to a ceasefire (4 February); negotiation and conclusion of the Plaka Armistice between ELAS and EDES (5–29 February).

11 March EAM-ELAS inaugurate the PEEA, without EDES or EKKA participation.

17–20 May Negotiation and conclusion of the Lebanon Agreement, signalling the formation of a National Unity Government and subsuming the PEEA.

6–25 June German forces conduct anti-partisan Operation *Gemsbock* in the border region between German-occupied Albania and north-western Greece.

July EDES re-opens hostilities against German forces around Parga and Arta (3 July); German forces launch Operation *Steinadler* against the ELAS bands around Pentalofos (3 July); the battle of Amfilochia between the ELAS 8th Division and elements of the 104. Jäger-Division (12 July); Oberkommando der Wehrmacht issues Directive 48, centralizing authority for the defence of the Balkans and reorganizing the German forces (26 July); 11-strong Soviet Mission, under Lieutenant-Colonel Grigori M. Popov, arrives in Greece (28 July).

August Two German companies, 2. and 3./SS-Polizei-Panzergrenadier-Regiment 8, launch Operation *Kreuzotter* against the EDES bands in the Mount Parnon area, near Amfissa, Central Greece; battle of Menina (Thesprotia), between EDES and elements of the 1. Gebirgs-Division, supported by Albanian irregulars (17–18 August); Heeresgruppe E orders the start of the evacuation of all German forces from Greece, except for the Crete and Rhodes garrisons (end of August).

September ELAS and EDES attempt to block the retreat of German forces, as part of Operation *Noah's Ark* (10 September); battle of Meligalas (Messinia) pits ELAS forces against collaborationist troops (13–14 September); conclusion of the Caserta Agreement between ELAS, EDES, the Greek government-in-exile and General Sir Henry M. Wilson, Supreme Allied Commander for the Mediterranean, leading to the creation of a united national army (26 September).

October German forces evacuate Athens (12 October) and Thessaloniki (30 October); Bulgarian forces evacuate Greece (25 October).

November Last of German forces evacuate Greece (2 November); battle of Kilkis, pitting ELAS against collaborationist forces in Northern Greece (3–4 November); the Greek 3rd Rimini Brigade lands in Greece (5 November).

ELAS: THE PAN-HELLENIC RESISTANCE ARMY

Command structure

EAM formally established the symbolically named ELAS (spelled with a double 'L', its name would have matched the Greek word for 'Greece'), its very own guerrilla army, in December 1942. Previously, it had controlled small armed bands, restricted to sporadic, uncoordinated and low-impact attacks. ELAS's General Headquarters (GHQ) only came into being in May 1943. Both ELAS GHQ and the lower commands originally operated under a triangular command structure, consisting of a military commander, a political adviser and a *kapetánios*. The military commander oversaw operations, while the *kapetánios* (his co-equal) was responsible for administration, recruitment, supplies, unit morale and political enlightenment. The overall military commander of ELAS was Colonel Stéfanos Saráfis, a militarily competent, latently anti-British and viscerally anti-Monarchist former Greek Army regular officer who, despite not being a Communist, had been won over to EAM's cause around the time of the establishment of ELAS GHQ (Colonel Dimitrios Psarros, a respected Republican military figure, and leader of the rival EKKA band, had earlier turned down EAM's invitation to take up that post). Until the abolition of the post of political adviser, the latter were the most important members of the ELAS command structure, and they also held ELAS officer rank. Following the abolition of that post in the spring of 1944, former political advisers were redeployed as chiefs-of-staff or other senior position-holders at lower levels of the ELAS command structure. The *Protokapetánios* (arch-captain) of ELAS was Aris Velouchiòtis, the *nom de guerre* of Athanasios Klaras, a ruthless, charismatic and organizationally adept veteran Communist, imprisoned, pre-war, for his political convictions, but also for criminal acts. Because only KKE cadres were eligible for the post of *kapetánios*, they eventually took over the political

An Orthodox priest on horseback heartily shakes the hand of a civilian, under the watchful eye of a smiling *andartis*, armed with a captured MP 40 submachine gun. The priest is himself a guerrilla, judging by his (pistol?) ammunition belt, hobnailed jackboots and the military greatcoat folded over the neck of his mount. Orthodox priests were present in all guerrilla bands, including ELAS (to which the priest portrayed here is most likely attached), officiating over ceremonies, preaching sermons, blessing the weapons of the guerrillas and even fighting alongside them. (Athens War Museum)

Colonel Saráfis, flanked by two members of his staff and shadowed by three youthful bodyguards. The smiling staff officers most likely bear the rank of *tagmatàrchis* (major), judging by the single, six-pointed metal star pinned on their former Greek Army tunics' shoulder straps, and on the side of their forage caps. The bodyguards are armed with .45 Thompson submachine guns, a status symbol among guerrillas and a suitable weapon for the security detail of none other than the ELAS military commander himself. Note that no two of the ELAS fighters shown here wear the same badge on their forage caps. (Athens War Museum)

advisers' role. In 1944 *kapetánioi* were granted reserve-officer status. At the apex of ELAS's strength, some 1,000 *kapetánioi* (symbolically named after the chieftains who led irregular bands during Greece's War of Independence) made up a sizeable share of the total ELAS officer corps.

Organization and recruitment

The creation of ELAS GHQ and the appointment of Saráfis as supreme military commander signalled ELAS's gradual reorganization into a regular army. In June 1943, ELAS GHQ controlled some 4,500 men in Macedonia, about 4,000 in Thessaly, 3,000 in Roumeli (central Greece) and roughly 500 in Epirus (the stronghold of ELAS's arch-rival, EDES). These regional forces were originally organized into *Archigeia* ('Headquarters') or *Genikes Dioikìseis* ('General Commands'), sub-divided into commands and sub-commands, respectively. In July 1943, ELAS GHQ reshuffled its organizational structure, giving regular army designations to all units with effect from 1 September 1943: headquarters and general commands became divisions, commands became regiments and subcommands battalions, with each of them divided into companies, platoons and sections. In truth, the strength of the ELAS divisions barely reached 4,000 men (or one-third of the conventional establishment of a division), with battalions composed of no more than 400 men. ELAS *andartes* spent most of their time in smaller units, dispersed across the countryside, and only assembled as full-strength units for larger-scale tactical operations.

To approximate the organizational structure of a regular military force, and to attain the discipline levels of a conventional army, ELAS instituted, as of mid 1943, military regulations: saluting became mandatory, and disciplinary measures (which included the death penalty for particularly egregious offences) were rigorously enforced, either locally (in urgent cases) or following the approval of the higher command. In 1944, regular courts-martial were established at divisional level. As with the members of any regular army, the men and women of ELAS were expected to swear an oath of allegiance and they became, as of the summer of 1943, eligible for moral awards and distinctions, as well as for promotion (including to reserve-officer status).

Members of the ELAS Thessaly Division pose for the camera in an assortment of uniforms. The weapons visible here are a .45 Thompson M1921 submachine gun with a barrel compensator and a drum-shaped magazine, as well as a .303 Bren light machine gun. Standing first and second from the right are Alvertos Amon and Pepos Kohen, both of the Jewish Community of the city of Volos. (© Photographic Archive – Jewish Museum of Greece)

ELAS rank-and-file guerrillas did not bear rank insignia; later in the war, most of its officers followed a rank designation system broadly inspired by that of the pre-war regular Greek Army. They also wore uniform items that denoted their hierarchically superior status, such as Sam Browne-style belts and knee-high riding boots and carried binocular or map-cases, daggers and whips. Despite its political leanings, ELAS did not fly banners featuring Communist symbols, unlike their counterparts in Yugoslavia and elsewhere in the Balkans: ELAS units only allowed the carrying of Greek national flags and the display of locally made devices and emblems on their uniforms, reminiscent in their choice of colours and overall composition, of pre-war national devices and emblems, ostensibly in a show of non-partisan patriotism, but, also, in a bid to put some distance between them and the KKE's Communist ideology.

ELAS recruited its rank and file from areas of the Greek countryside under its control. Given that ELAS held sway over large swathes of rural Greece, its recruitment base was substantial. Although ELAS did recruit some of its men forcibly, most were volunteers, with the number of fresh recruits joining its ranks increasing as the prospect of Germany's defeat loomed larger. From a strength of fewer than 5,000 men in the spring of 1943, ELAS boasted close to 20,000 men by the autumn of the same

A troop of the ELAS Cavalry Brigade charges forward, most likely in Thessaly. This photograph was probably taken in the aftermath of Italy's surrender to the Allies in September 1943, which saw ELAS inherit most of the mounts and equipment of the Reggimento 'Lancieri di Aosta' (6°). The ELAS cavalrymen shown here appear to carry Italian 6.5mm Mannlicher-Carcano M1891 cavalry carbines, and their overall appearance is surprisingly uniform for a guerrilla army. (Unknown/ Wikimedia/Public Domain)

ELAS cadres review a parading troop, in a photograph taken between mid-1943 and late 1944. Despite its humble beginnings, ELAS developed into the most disciplined of all Greek guerrilla bands, and by the time of the conclusion of the National Resistance, it had come close to observing regular Army organizational standards. (Athens War Museum)

year; the estimates of Colonel E.C.W. Myers stood at 16,000 *andartes* for the regular ELAS units and 16,000 more in the ELAS armed reserves. Between the spring of 1944 and Greece's liberation, ELAS dominated the Greek resistance movement: in November 1944, ELAS's regular force stood at about 70,000 *andartes*, forming ten divisions, supported by a further 50,000 in the ELAS armed reserves. By that stage, ELAS GHQ had assumed army status, while intermediate headquarters or *Omádes Merarhíon* (so-called 'groups of divisions') had also been formed (for the ELAS order of battle, see page 13). Members of EPON, EAM's youth groups, had also been integrated into the ELAS divisions with one so-called 'model EPON platoon' for each regiment and one model group for each battalion.

As ELAS grew, so too did its needs for officers, who were recruited from two main pools. The first was composed of former regular Greek Army officers who took to the mountains to fight against the Axis occupiers, including some who had originally joined competing guerrilla factions. After ELAS liquidated Psarros's EKKA in the spring of 1944, many of its officers joined ELAS; Saráfis himself only joined ELAS after his own guerrilla band, AAA, had been similarly liquidated. By the time of Greece's liberation, some 800 former regular Greek Army officers (from the days of the Greek monarchy) and some 1,500 more of Republican convictions had joined ELAS, making up around 45 per cent of its entire officer corps. The second source of officer recruitment was ELAS's own cadet-officer training school, established in July 1943 at Redina in the Agrafa Mountains. The school's first class of junior lieutenants graduated in late September 1943 and, by the time of liberation in October 1944, some 1,270 reserve officers – one-quarter of ELAS's entire officer corps – had graduated from the school.

Communications were a major shortcoming of the ELAS bands. Originally ensured through couriers, communications often proved unreliable, especially in emergencies, forcing ELAS to turn to field telephones. In the summer of 1943, every ELAS division received orders to establish a communications company and every regiment a communications platoon. By August 1943, direct telephone communications had been established between ELAS GHQ and each of the four ELAS divisions then in existence. For all their merits, telephone communications proved unreliable when they were needed the most, such as during enemy mopping-up operations, in the early stages of which the Axis forces prioritized the disruption of

A group of BLOs photographed somewhere in Greece's mountains in 1943 or 1944. Except when they infiltrated urban settlements, BLOs wore their regular home unit uniforms, to avoid forsaking the Hague Convention protections if taken prisoner. Their British Army uniforms also doubled as symbols of authority vis-à-vis the *andartes*, who were more willing to defer to those visibly serving with the prestigious British Army. (Athens War Museum)

telephone wires. To address this concern, ELAS GHQ turned to radio communications, seeking to emulate the example of the British Liaison Officers (BLOs), who invariably travelled around the Greek countryside with radio operators in their midst, to be able to liaise directly with Middle East Command. By the time of Greece's liberation, all ELAS divisions possessed and used radio sets.

ELAS largely relied on pack animals to transport its supplies, as motor transport was something of a rarity in wartime Greece, especially in the rugged countryside. The pack animals used were made available by the locals, mostly without the expectation of pecuniary reward (ELAS *andartes* are known to have shared their rations with the animal handlers and furnished animal fodder).

Finally, a word on rations. Since Greece was, even in peacetime, a food-importing country, feeding sizeable guerrilla forces remained a challenge throughout the National Resistance. Foodstuffs were procured locally, either through requisitioning or through purchase, with ELAS having established its own price-scale for their acquisition.

Weapons and personal equipment

ELAS procured its weapons and ammunition through three main sources: war booty, Allied supply drops and, following Italy's surrender to the Allies in September 1943, the former Italian occupation forces' stocks (those not surrendered to, or taken by, the Germans). Ammunition was in scarce supply, however, chronically impeding both operations and training. Clothing and shoes were also not available in sufficient quantities, which explains the motley appearance of ELAS guerrillas. The main sources of clothing and shoes were stocks of pre-war regular Greek Army uniforms, air-dropped Allied supplies (mostly British battledress), locally requisitioned clothing and uniform items manufactured in guerrilla workshops. Clothing and boots were also taken from fallen or captured enemy troops. Italy's surrender would prove something of a boon, also in this respect. Cold-weather clothes were, generally, in even shorter supply, with many cases of frostbite reported among ELAS personnel.

Saráfis and his retinue review a line-up of ELAS *andartes*, most likely in the spring of 1944. The youthful looks of the men he salutes suggest that these could be members of EPON, the ELAS youth organization, on the occasion of their integration into an ELAS combat unit. What is noteworthy is their uniform appearance and their disciplined turnout, two of the main achievements of Saráfis during his tenure as ELAS commander. (Athens War Museum)

ELAS naval forces

Although it had no air assets, ELAS was the only Greek guerrilla band to boast a (modest) naval arm, in service between 1942 and 1945. The essentially coastal fleet fielded by ELAN consisted of armed motor sailing vessels of over 7kts speed, with a loading capacity of around 10 tons and a crew of up to 18 men; smaller, armed motor crafts with a loading capacity of up to 10 tons and a crew of up to 12 men; and other, unarmed transportation craft. ELAN's armed fleet formed seven squadrons of up to four flotillas each, and one autonomous flotilla of six vessels. These operated under the overall command of ELAS GHQ but were attached to the ELAS divisions in whose jurisdiction their shore bases belonged. ELAN's final tally reached roughly 100 motor vessels – several of which boasted a displacement of over 200 tons – operated by a force of 1,200 officers, *kapetánioi* and guerrillas. ELAN carried out both offensive actions (harassment and plundering of enemy transport, and escort of ELAS convoys) and logistical support missions (transfer of friendly forces, food, equipment, and supplies, including between Pelion (Greece) and neighbouring Turkey).

ELAS order of battle, end of November 1944

Regular ELAS (total establishment: 67,000 men), as follows:
Macedonia Group of divisions: four divisions (13 regiments, 12,500 men)
Roumeli Group of divisions: two divisions (six regiments, 11,500 men)
One army corps in Athens/Piraeus (six regiments and one car company, 9,000 men)
Peloponnese division (five regiments, 11,000 men)
Thessaly division (four regiments, 9,000 men)
Epirus division (six regiments, 5,000 men)
Cretan division (three regiments, 4,000 men)
Aegean Islands Brigade (two regiments, one each on Lesbos and Samos, 3,000 men)
Cavalry Brigade (two regiments, 1,500 men)
GHQ Guard Battalion (500 men)
In addition, there were ELAN (1,200 men); National Guard (10,800 men); and the ELAS armed reserves (50,000 men).

EDES: THE JUNIOR RESISTANCE ARMY

Organization and command structure

EDES was originally founded as a political resistance movement and, by mid-1942, it had found a commander-in-chief for its guerrilla arm: Colonel Napoleon Zervas, a former regular Greek Army officer of Republican convictions dismissed in the 1930s for earlier subversive activities and, like many, denied the possibility of joining in Greece's defence during the Greco-Italian War. After Britain had committed to support EDES, Zervas took to the mountains (even if only reluctantly), at the head of only a handful of *andartes*. When Lieutenant-Colonel Myers first met Zervas in November 1942, the latter commanded a modest 150 men, of whom one-third took part in the Gorgopotamos River railway bridge sabotage on 24–25 November. By early 1943, EDES had expanded to about 600 *andartes*; by April 1943 to 1,000; and by the summer of the same year to an estimated 5,000, backed by an equal number of EDES armed reservists.

Napoleon Zervas, commander-in-chief and leader of EDES. Following a distinguished military career, which included his participation in the Balkan Wars and World War I, he became involved in political intrigue during the 1920s, which cost him his commission and put a premature end to his progression to higher office. Zervas closely aligned himself with the British during the National Resistance, becoming an instrument for the pursuit of their policies in Greece. After the end of World War II, he formed his own political party, entered parliament and held ministerial office. He withdrew from politics in 1951 and died in Athens on 10 December 1957. (Athens War Museum)

Until the summer of 1943, EDES operated small guerrilla bands led by junior but capable officers possessed of considerable independence within their area of operational responsibility. As it grew, EDES reorganized its forces, recasting them into more formal military formations: by July 1943, EDES had established up to ten (understrength) divisions or smaller tactical units of two regiments each. Each regiment consisted of two (understrength) battalions, with a total establishment of about 1,000. The EDES headquarters and the bulk of these forces were in Epirus, with smaller groups operating in Thessaly and the Peloponnese.

Despite the establishment, at the behest of the Allies, and the short-lived operation of a combined Greek guerrilla forces headquarters, opposing political views soon brought ELAS and EDES into open conflict. By late 1943, EDES had been all but destroyed by ELAS, bringing the latter closer to its avowed goal of monopolizing the armed resistance movement. To counterbalance the preponderance of ELAS, Britain increased its support to EDES and discontinued its supplies to ELAS. In mid-1944, with the German forces' withdrawal approaching, the British also sent Greek reinforcements from the Middle East to help replenish the fledgling EDES. By midsummer 1944, taking advantage of the Plaka Armistice (29 February 1944), which put an end to inter-guerrilla hostilities, EDES reached a ceiling of 12,000 *andartes* organized in four divisions. In the autumn of 1944, after their final mopping-up operations in response to the guerrilla offensive (Operation *Noah's Ark*), the Germans estimated the strength of EDES at about 8,000 men.

EDES, which, in July 1943, had changed its name to EOEA, at the suggestion of the British, to signal the break with its formerly anti-Monarchist political stance, remained throughout the creature of Zervas, its military leader, who, in turn, owed the existence of his guerrilla movement to British support. After EDES had reneged on its former Republican agenda, the association between Zervas and the British became even closer, to the point that the EDES headquarters was subordinated to Middle East Command and to the British-sponsored Greek government-in-exile, which was loyal to exiled King George II of the Hellenes.

Recruitment base

Following Zervas's declaration for King George II of the Hellenes in March 1943, EDES's political credibility with pro-Monarchist circles increased. As a result, many pro-Monarchist former regular Greek Army officers flocked to the mountains, swelling the ranks of EDES. Many of them were, politically, right-wing and, in some cases, not immune to charges of collaboration. Although it is difficult to establish Zervas's personal complicity in collaboration, there is some circumstantial evidence to corroborate that charge against him, some of it provided by

Captain Christos Papadatos (at left), chief-of-staff of the EDES Epirus headquarters, and 2nd Lieutenant Marios Maniakis give a leg up to a British NCO (a radio operator), in October 1943. BLOs invariably travelled around the Greek countryside in the company of their radio operator(s), who played a crucial role in maintaining contact between Middle East Command in Cairo and the Greek guerrilla bands affiliated to the Allied cause. (Athens War Museum)

Two EDES officers (on the left, Captain Gheorghios Agoros) flank a smiling BLO, somewhere in the mountains of Greece, during the Axis occupation of Greece. (Athens War Museum)

Studio portrait of two EDES *andartes*, photographed in November 1944, just days after the withdrawal of the last German troops from Thessaloniki. They are both turned out in battledress, and wear *Evzoni*-like moulded fezzes (without the characteristic black tassel). As they display no visible insignia, it is difficult to identify their rank. The meaning of their shoulder cords is unclear, but these are likely to designate their function rather than their rank. The man standing on the right also displays an unidentified decoration ribbon. (Athens War Museum)

none other than General der Gebirgstruppe Hubert Lanz, commander of the XXII. Gebirgskorps. What is undisputed is that, between October 1943 and June 1944, a 'silent truce' was in place between EDES and the Germans, who had invested in Zervas's neutrality and attributed to Allied coercion his subsequent re-opening of hostilities against them.

Below the level of its officer corps, EDES recruited its members from among the peasants and mountain populations, similarly to ELAS. Kinship, personal allegiance to the recruiter, local specificities or pure luck determined which of the rival factions a recruit joined. Allied supplies (which included gold sovereigns) also proved an invaluable incentive for EDES recruitment, both because they conferred the prestige of Allied recognition and because they promised fresh recruits a less precarious existence to the one that the more destitute among them eked out in their native villages. EDES is not known to have used force to recruit peasants to its cause, with recruitment boosted by the aura of the Gorgopotamos sabotage operation and the brutal reprisals to which the Axis occupiers increasingly resorted to obstruct the growth of the resistance movement. Following the Plaka Armistice, recruitment for EDES was limited to within the boundaries of the area it controlled (Epirus). As this was relatively small and sparsely populated, the mass that EDES could hope to attain was limited and, although its strength fluctuated, it was always considerably smaller than ELAS.

Weapons and personal equipment

Not unlike their ELAS counterparts, EDES guerrillas wore a mix of military and civilian clothing items, including moulded fezzes made of felt, woollen

Four EDES officers (from left to right, Captain Dimitrios Georghiadis, Captain Gheorghios Agoros, Captain Christos Papadatos and Reserve 2nd Lieutenant Katsiaounis) in a photograph taken at the EDES-controlled port of Splantza (present-day Ammoudia, in the vicinity of Parga), most likely in 1943, on the occasion of an Allied delivery of supplies. The BLOs considered EDES to be tactically superior to rival guerrilla bands, at least in early 1943, thanks to the formal training of its former regular Greek Army officers. (Athens War Museum)

shepherds' coats and indigenous kilts. EDES shared much the same sources of personal equipment as ELAS, making it difficult to distinguish between EDES and ELAS *andartes* in period photographs. The rival bands also shared the same sources of weapons, with EDES guerrillas carrying a similar assortment of Greek, Italian and German-made rifles, and British, German and Italian-made automatic weapons as their ELAS counterparts. One notable difference between these two partisan armies was that, from the summer of 1944, EDES was equipped with some heavier weapons, in the form of mountain artillery pieces (see page 18), delivered by boat to the western Greece sea ports, such as Parga, that EDES controlled. Significantly, the British kept up their weapons supplies to EDES throughout the occupation, allowing its command to counterbalance its numerical inferiority to ELAS with a qualitative parity.

Group photograph of a company of EDES *andartes* in the aftermath of an engagement with German forces in the Tzoumerka Mountains (Epirus), in the autumn of 1943. Their weapons include three 6.5mm Breda 30 light machine guns (the Italian armed forces' poorly designed standard squad weapon during World War II), and one 8mm Breda 37 medium machine gun (in the foreground, left, resting on a tripod). These weapons would have been taken over from their former Italian owners, following Italy's exit from World War II, and briefly used against the Germans until EDES's informal truce with General der Gebirgstruppe Hubert Lanz's troops in October 1943. (Athens War Museum)

Colonel Zervas, accompanied by some of his men, holds a discussion with British naval or Royal Marine officers on the occasion of the delivery to EDES, by sea, of Allied supplies. It has been suggested that the bearded man standing next to Zervas in what looks like a British Army uniform is Dragolijub 'Draža' Mihailović, leader of the non-Communist Yugoslav Resistance (Chetnik) movement. Although it is true that the two men had sought to establish contact and meet in Epirus, there is no evidence that they ever actually met. (Athens War Museum)

GUERRILLA TRAINING, TACTICS AND OPERATIONS

ELAS and EDES recruits with previous military experience were trained for up to a week, typically on a unit-by-unit basis down to platoon level, with an emphasis on small-arms handling, use and basic repair. Those without military experience attended courses lasting between two and four weeks, during which they were taught drill and weapons handling as well as mine laying and the planting of demolition charges. Tactical training mostly took place on smaller-scale operations against 'softer' enemy targets. The intensity and quality of training depended on two factors: first, the ability and initiative of local commanders; and second, the need to field fresh troops for participation in actual operations. Training also included some political indoctrination, which, one suspects, would have occupied

Surrounded by members of his staff, Colonel Zervas proudly inspects a battery of US-made 75mm pack howitzers on M1 carriages. Despite being the junior resistance grouping, EDES was the only partisan army in wartime Greece to field mountain artillery pieces, delivered to it by sea after the fall of southern Italy to the Allies. (Athens War Museum)

Fighters of ELAS's X Division are trained on the use of mines by Lieutenant Livingstone (centre) and a second unidentified member of the British Military Mission in Dasochori, Grevena (Western Macedonia), in August 1944. (Iason Chandrinos Collection)

a larger part of the training schedule of ELAS fighters. Allied Military Mission reports concur that the overall level of training of the average rank-and-file *andartis* left something to be expected: fire discipline was less than ideal and unit coordination standards not too high. What Greek *andartes* lacked in those respects, however, they made up for in tenacity and, for many, in near-fanatical bravery.

The tactic most widely deployed was the ambush. Following an ambush, guerrilla units would withdraw to their mountain sanctuaries, while reservists would melt back into the civilian population. Other favoured guerrilla operations included the laying of mines and the planting of demolition charges, mostly by night, to disrupt transportation routes and lines of communication (notably, railway lines, tunnels and telephone wires), causing casualties and tying down enemy security and engineer personnel. From September 1943 onwards, a great deal of the explosives used for guerrilla demolition work were salvaged from unexploded ordnance (including sea mines) left behind by the Italians, following Italy's surrender. So-called 'stone mines' (pressure-type explosive devices with a non-metallic casing, built to resemble stones) were put to good

Cadet officers attend a mortar training course at the ELAS officers' school in Redina (Agrafa Mountains) in the summer of 1944. The mortar shown here is an 81mm weapon of Italian manufacture. (Iason Chandrinos Collection)

use in Greece as they were simple enough for the average *andartis* to use, and difficult for the occupation forces to detect amid the rock-strewn terrain. Sniping at individual soldiers, unguarded car columns, isolated vehicles and small enemy parties was also commonplace, making the Greek countryside a dangerous place for the enemy. Larger-scale actions at the initiative of the *andartes* were less commonplace and, when they did occur, they were violent but brief, typically followed by longer periods of operational inactivity.

One of the less savoury aspects of the *andartes*' behaviour was their contempt for the rules that governed the conduct of war. There is ample evidence to suggest that Greek *andartes* routinely tortured their prisoners, less to extract information

The aftermath of the Gorgopotamos River railway bridge sabotage operation on 24–25 November 1942, one of the most spectacular and strategically significant sabotage actions anywhere in occupied Europe during World War II. The success of the SOE-planned operation, which resulted in the flow of supplies to Rommel's Deutsches Afrikakorps being discontinued for six weeks, persuaded the British to invest in Greece's resistance movement. The latter came to depend on Allied support, allowing the British and, later, the Americans, to harness it in pursuit of their wartime objectives and longer-term geo-strategic aspirations. (Athens War Museum)

and more as a sport: prisoner abuse, mutilation and execution were commonplace in Greece's mountains. Attacks on unprotected enemy ambulances and hospital trains were also not unheard of. These acts of savagery attracted vengeful Axis retaliation, mostly against innocent civilians, feeding the cycle of blood and intensifying the mutual sense of hatred between the oppressed and their oppressors.

Larger-scale guerrilla operations in Greece were mandated and coordinated by the Special Operations Executive (SOE). The first major operation in which Greek *andartes* participated, under British command, was the blasting of the Gorgopotamos River railway bridge, one of the largest sabotage operations in occupied Europe and one of the most fateful, as it would persuade the British to invest in armed subversion, as opposed to political opposition, across occupied Europe. The second major operation began in June 1943, when SOE mandated the Greek *andartes* to launch Operation *Animals*, a sustained, two-month-long campaign of ambushes, convoy attacks and communication network disruptions, to mislead the Germans into believing that an Allied invasion of Greece was imminent. Operation *Animals* was a success, causing significant damage to the Axis forces and deflecting some of their attention and resources from the Allies' true objective, the island of Sicily. Major guerrilla operations resumed between July and October 1944, as part of Operation *Noah's Ark*, to harass the Axis forces during their 1,600km-long retreat towards the central and western Balkans. Although it did hold up the German retreat, causing attrition to the occupation forces, Operation *Noah's Ark* did not impede the orderly withdrawal of the German troops, which had been completed by November 1944.

GERMAN OCCUPATION FORCES

Organization and occupation record

An attack on Greece was not in Hitler's original plans, and it may have never materialized had it not been for Italy's failed invasion, in October 1940, which damaged the reputation of the Axis, and for the subsequent stationing of some British troops (including air assets) on Greek territory, which exposed Germany's flank to the threat of attacks on Romania, a major source of fuel for Germany's war machine during World War II. After they had overpowered Greece, the Germans planned to occupy the country with only a limited contingent of troops. By the autumn of 1943 this had become an impossibility due to the surrender of their Italian allies, which temporarily left much of rural Greece in the hands of the *andartes*. This event forced the Germans to take on the role of Greece's main occupation force, at a time when the Allies were spreading rumours of an imminent landing in western Greece or the Aegean Sea islands. These rumours were taken seriously by the Germans and their Bulgarian allies, even after the Allied landings on Sicily (Operation *Husky*), in July–August 1943. What is also worth noting is that, in the early stages of their occupation of Greece, the Germans were more favourably disposed vis-à-vis the Greeks compared to many other occupied peoples and, especially, the Slavs, whom the Germans regarded as racially inferior and lacking in culture. As World War II wore on, however, and with the Greek resistance movement becoming more assertive, the Germans hardened their stance, unleashing a campaign of reprisals that would cost the lives of tens of thousands of civilians (including hostages, Communist sympathizers, and saboteurs, actual or presumed) and the destruction of hundreds of villages and settlements across the country.

The German occupation forces in Greece chronically suffered from two shortcomings, both of which had an adverse effect on their coordination and overall efficiency, especially at the level of intelligence sharing and exploitation: first, their inadequate numbers and, second,

BELOW LEFT
A smartly dressed German infantry officer and several NCOs pose for the camera on the deck of a troop-transport vessel, en route to Crete. Despite the Axis efforts, Greek waters were never safe against submarine, surface-vessel and airborne attacks, forcing the occupying forces to adopt the practice of pre-emptive safety vest-wearing for those travelling by boat along the Aegean and the Ionian seas. (Author's Collection)

BELOW RIGHT
German troops line up for inspection along the pier at Piraeus port, en route to North Africa. The closer Generalfeldmarschall Erwin Rommel's Deutsches Afrikakorps came to the Suez Canal, the greater the importance of Greece to the Germans, who relied heavily on the country's underdeveloped road and railway network, as well as on its ports and airports, to transport men and supplies to North Africa. (Author's Collection)

their complex organization, characterized by a multitude of commands exercising overlapping responsibilities. Responsibility for the occupation of Greece was assigned to Heeresgruppe E (Generaloberst Alexander Löhr), which was part of Oberbefehlshaber Südost (Generalfeldmarschall Maximilian von Weichs). Unusually, no 'armies' were subordinate to Heeresgruppe E, which, in the autumn of 1943, consisted of two corps: the LXVIII. Armeekorps (General der Flieger Hellmuth Felmy) and the XXII. Gebirgskorps (General der Gebirgstruppe Hubert Lanz). The former was responsible for securing and defending eastern Greece and most of the Peloponnese, while the latter oversaw the security and defence of western Greece, from Epirus to the Gulf of Patras. Besides the tactical organization of Heeresgruppe E, there was a German military administration – Militärbefehlshaber Griechenland (General der Flieger Wilhelm Speidel) – that was not subordinate to Heeresgruppe E but, instead, to the Militärbefehlshaber Südost (Belgrade). The problem of overlapping competences was exacerbated by the creation, around the time of Italy's surrender, of the post of *Höherer SS- und Polizei-Führer* for Greece (Generalleutnant der Waffen-SS Walter Schimana) who, although notionally subordinate to Speidel, in fact operated under the control of Reichsführer-SS Heinrich Himmler, and by the presence in Greece of a special plenipotentiary (Hermann Neubacher), who represented the interests of Germany's Ministry of Economics and Ministry for Foreign Affairs.

Turning to the question of their qualitative and quantitative adequacy, German troops stationed in Greece were estimated at around 140,000 at the end of 1943, and just over 100,000 in August 1944, broken down into six divisions and several smaller-sized formations (for the German occupation forces' order of battle, see page 24). Some of those formations were front-line, combat-ready troops, as in the case of the 1. Gebirgs-Division and the 4. SS-Polizei-Panzergrenadier-Division, while others were either second-rate troops, only suitable for garrison and stationary defence duties, on account of the advanced age or poor physical condition of their men or were otherwise deemed unreliable (as in the case of the non-German troops stationed in Greece, which included Armenian, Arab and Turkic forces). The shortage of tough and reliable troops was only (partly) addressed as of late 1943, with the increasing recruitment and use of locally raised collaborationist forces (a topic touched on in more detail later in this study). If the forces available to the Germans were never sufficient to fully secure the key infrastructures facilitating the unobstructed transport and distribution of troops and supplies across Greece or to pacify the countryside, they would prove just about enough to keep the *andartes* from overrunning the major urban centres and liberating Greece.

Anti-partisan tactics and operations

To address the intensifying Resistance problem in Greece, the Germans relied on a combination of major and smaller-scale anti-partisan actions in the mountains of Greece. The Germans used the term *Banditenbekämpfung* ('anti-brigand') to describe those actions, betraying their contempt for partisan forces, and a certain misunderstanding regarding their level of organization. To conduct smaller-scale anti-partisan operations the Germans made tactical use of so-called *Jagdkommandos* (hunting parties), previously used in Yugoslavia and the Soviet Union: these were small-sized detachments made up of younger and physically fit men, with prior combat experience, who would 'go native', to detect concentrations of *andartes*. Once they had detected their 'prey', the *Jagdkommandos* would either eliminate it themselves or ask for reinforcements, if the partisan forces were too large or too well dug in.

Efficient as they were, *Jagdkommandos* did not suffice to stem the tide of the armed resistance movement. As a result, the Germans also launched, starting in 1943, several larger-scale 'mopping-up' anti-partisan operations (see the Chronology section of this book). The tactical manoeuvre that the Germans deployed when conducting those operations was the encirclement, through two, roughly concentric circles, one outer, cast wide and more thinly manned, and one inner,

Studio portrait of a *Gebirgsjäger*, with the rank of an *Obergefreiter* – see the double upper-sleeve chevron embroidered in silver thread against a dark background – most likely photographed post-1943. *Gebirgsjäger* were among the most formidable German Army formations to be stationed in Greece during World War II. One of the major successes of the Greek resistance was to tie down such élite Wehrmacht formations, which, if available for use on other fronts, could have helped to turn, be it only temporarily, the tide of war in Germany's favour. (Author's Collection)

manned by the more combat-ready and physically fit elements. Both circles were gradually tightened, until the guerrillas in the encirclement were pushed into a 'pocket', small enough for a final assault, to eliminate or capture them.

Before conducting larger-scale operations, the Germans would meticulously gather intelligence and assemble tactical data, through use of their network of spies, camouflaged observation posts, tactical air reconnaissance, the monitoring of the guerrilla bands' radio communications, the tapping of their telephone lines and the interrogation of prisoners or suspected guerrilla sympathizers. To preserve confidentiality and to throw the *andartes* off the scent of an impending mopping-up operation, the Germans would also spread misinformation (including among their own troops) or make visible preparations for dummy (cover-up) operations. In those cases where an area of encirclement contained villages or other, major settlements, these were carefully reconnoitred and, typically, approached through an enveloping manoeuvre, to avoid death traps for the German troops.

Although it was not unusual for the *andartes* to evade capture (often by lying low) or to altogether escape enemy encirclement during mopping-up operations, especially under cover of darkness or by exploiting temporary gaps in the encirclements, these operations were, by and large, successful at eliminating considerable numbers of guerrillas: Operations *Wulf*, *Horrido* and *Rentier* alone, resulted in some 1,000 *andartes* killed and 500 being taken prisoner. That said, major anti-partisan operations were also costly for the Germans, in *matériel* and personnel alike, and, for all the planning and resources that went into them, they never achieved the goal of eradicating the guerrilla problem in Greece. It is telling that, in July and August 1944, the Germans suffered some 940 killed, 1,230 wounded and 280 missing in fighting against the guerrilla bands. Perhaps the most significant success of the German anti-partisan operations was to keep open the north–south railway line that connected Athens to Thessaloniki long enough to allow for the evacuation of the bulk of their forces – except for the garrisons in Rhodes and Crete, which were left behind to fend for themselves. The last of the German troops to be evacuated from Greece crossed into Yugoslavia on 2 November 1944, ending the painful chapter of Greece's occupation, in anticipation of the formal opening of the Greek Civil War, on 31 March 1946.

German occupation forces' order of battle, 20 August 1944

(Heeresgruppe E and Militärbefehlshaber Griechenland, estimated at 100,000 troops)

Heeresgruppe E

Kommandant Ost-Ägäis: Festungs-Brigade 939; Küstenjäger-Abteilung 'Brandenburg'; Artillerie-Regiment 627; Sturm-Division Rhodos; Panzer-Abteilung Rhodos; Panzer-Aufklärungs-Abteilung 999; Festungs-Brigade 967; Festungs-Brigade 968

Kommandant der Festung Kreta: 133. Festungs-Division; 22. Luftlande Infanterie-Division; Artillerie-Regiment Kreta

LXVIII. Armeekorps: 41. Festungs-Division; 117. Jäger-Division; 11. Luftwaffen-Felddivision; Sicherungs-Regiment 86

XXII. Gebirgskorps: 1. Gebirgs-Division; 104. Jäger-Division; Festungs-Brigade 964; Festungs-Brigade 966; Festungs-Brigade 1017

LXXXXI. Armeekorps: 4. SS-Polizei-Panzergrenadier-Division; Festungs-Brigade 963; Festungs-Brigade 969; Sicherungs-Regiment 639; Sicherungs-Regiment 91; Landesschützen-Regiment 81; Didymoteicho Regiment

Other commands in Greece (not under Heeresgruppe E): Militärbefehlshaber Griechenland; Marinebefehlshaber Griechenland; Kommandierender General der Deutschen Luftwaffe in Griechenland; 19. Flak-Division

(continued on page 33)

RESISTANCE LEADERS
1: Protokapetánios Aris Velouchiòtis, ELAS GHQ, Lamia, October 1944
2: Antistrátigos Stéfanos Saráfis, Caserta, Naples, September 1944
3: Syntagmatàrchis Napoleon Zervas, Derviziani, November 1942

A

RESISTANCE FORCES (1)
1: *Dioikitìs tagmatos*, ELAS, Amfissa, June 1944
2: *Mavroskoufis*, ELAS, Viniani, October 1943
3: *Andartissa*, 34th Parnassus Regiment, ELAS, Dervenochoria, October 1943

B

RESISTANCE FORCES (2)
1: *Dioikitìs tagmatos*, Athens Division, ELAS, October 1944
2: *Aetópoulo*, ELAS, Paramythia, April 1944
3: *Andartis*, 24th Regiment, EDES, Splantza, October 1943

RESISTANCE FORCES (3)
1: SOE liaison officer, Roumeli, May 1943
2: *Dioikitis tagmatos*, 40th Regiment, EDES, Derviziani, April 1943
3: *Andartis*, 2nd Regiment, ELAS, Thebes, November 1944

D